TIERRA HOLMES

Voices Within Range

VOICES

WITHIN RANGE

a collection of poetic narratives

by

Tierra Holmes

Holmes Publishing

Voices Within Range: A Collection of Poetic Narratives
 by Tierra Holmes

The narratives within this book are based on the author's recreation of factual and fictitious events (including characters and settings). The author reserves the right to express her personal experiences and ideas with reference to any people or places known or unknown, real or imagined/explicitly mentioned or implied.

Holmes Publishing
Printed in the United States of America (USA)
First Edition: December 2021

ISBN: 9798467945453

Author's official website can be found here Linktr.ee/Tierrah

For the writers who doubt the value of their stories, who wonder if their words are enough, who question if their vernacular is acceptable, who struggle with being imperfect, who fear being misunderstood, and decide to write anyway.

TABLE OF CONTENTS

Author's Note

The initial description of this book concealed a fundamental truth — about 80% of the poetic narratives shared *are* about me; they're based on my personal experiences and observations. You see, I create poetry based on my current reality, my understanding of past events, my visions for the future, my questions about society, my interactions with people, and more. As a creative writer, my goal is to retell what was, what is, and what could be.

In the beginning of my writing process, I'm usually reacting to something that triggers me and then compels me to express how I feel. Sometimes I place myself back in that moment and explore how I would react if the moment continued. Other times, new speakers/characters emerge as if they were there with me. But then my characters/speakers begin to dictate the story as if it was never my story to begin with. So, although my poetic narratives start with me and my truth, they don't always end with me – they are simply extensions of me.

And I felt it was necessary to add this note because a part of me is still afraid to be fully seen. But I understand that I can't encourage others to be courageous and accepting of self if I'm not willing to do the same. Writing and publishing this book was the ultimate act of self-love and self-validation; it was an opportunity for me to embrace my ideas and stand behind my own creations.

Tierra

VOICES
WITHIN RANGE

Acceptance

Acceptance

Should be easy to receive
It should be an incentive
For showing up as you are
Both unfiltered and unguarded
Willing to be seen unmasked
And willing to embrace others
In their bare skin

Sing, Sing Your Song

Your note is JOY
There was a time when you found joy in the little things.
You would laugh at simple jokes, dance on thin patches of grass, and dig your toes into the cool earth. Somedays, you would speak to familiar faces in the clouds, oblivious to whoever may be watching.

Your note is LOVE
There was a time when you were unapologetic.
You would bite your nails in public and roll your eyes at the sadiddy chicks. You would deepen your voice and out-boy the boys. You would race until you ran out of breath. You would shoot basketballs from a self-made 3-point line, feeling the magic in your fingers with every bucket.

Your note is FAITH
There was a time when airballs didn't faze you.
You would jump from green-box to green-box feeling the electricity in your knees with every leap and landing. The possibility of falling was both terrifying and exciting.

If only you knew there was a power source beneath your feet. Maybe you would have jumped a little bit higher. Maybe you would have reached beyond the vision you settled for. Maybe you would have been more eager to fly.

Your note is DOUBT
There was a time when you were afraid.
You would make the same decision twice. You would look for examples of success in any area but the one you cared for. You would remember saving pennies for a feast under-ground.

You would play hide-and-go- seek but never come out of hiding. You would normalize the darkness and shun the light. You would forget your purpose on purpose … just to avoid the airballs. Your search for a safety net made you the fish and the fisherman.

Your note is GRATITUDE

There is a time when you return to yourself.

When you recognize your own face. When you appreciate your mountains and your valleys. When you sing your own praises on key. When your river flows from truth. And when your spirit surrenders to its own song.

R.E.A.C.H: REinventing an Authentic Character through Healing

Once drowning in high expectations
and negative beliefs
This black woman is resurfacing
She's reimagining herself as a Queen
— Powerful, Intentional, and Serene —
A woman with a clear destiny

She's reaching for her first breath and a new taste
of freedom

Unlatching her spirit from low self-esteem
Unbounding her hands with free will
Unlocking her aspirations from a mental cage
Unshackling her ankles from acidic chains

She's reaching for her first breath and a new taste
of freedom

Unleashing her dignity from Shame and Guilt
Unknotting her neck from a metallic noose
Unclasping her vision from Confusion's fog
Unbinding her tongue from curses she spoke
upon herself

She's reaching for her first breath and a new taste
of freedom

REACH GIRL, REACH !!

Imperfection is Queen

She walks high and mighty even in busted shoes
Does ballet in Rainbow boots beneath a scorching sun
She leaps across puddles of muddy water in silver stilettos
That promise her sanctuary and sophistication

She lands on land with her palms face down
Finding the rugged earth too stubborn to bend or break
She puts makeup on a calloused face hoping to disguise
The ugliness that wears her face like a crown

She tries, with all her might, to soften the arrival of *Her*
The one they call Imperfection, the one they call Queen
The one who screams when her lashes fall or her pre-plucked wig
Slides down her back and into the seat that reeks of insecurities

Imperfection is the shy bitch who sings like a Supreme
In exchange for applause and encouragement of her dreams
She's someone unbecoming and meek, someone you ignore
Because she's important to see but not necessary to meet

And she knows this, but to be accepted is *still* her wish
So, she dances in public to a tune she's never heard, performing
As Confidence in a space where Confidence would never be
Pretending the next step in the routine is the one she completes
Ignoring the hundreds of eyes that agree her feet are moving off beat
They're mimicking Perfection when Perfection never asked to be seen

The community loved her more when she danced in the rain with her
Hair untamed and the brightest smile stretched across her face. She
Was original back in those days, the spitting image of herself. And the
People she wanted to please were already pleased with her. She didn't
Have to beg for their attention because they knew her name was
Imperfection.

Affirmations

Affirmations

Should be straight to the point
They should inspire you to drop the act
And become the beast that you are
They should expose the light in you
That *you* always knew existed

I Am: A Self-Love Affirmation

I am empowered to create a better life for ME. I have enough joy and love to give to myself and to others. I have gifts that inspire and empower people to believe in better days. I have power over my mind.

I am a
Multi-Genius
I am a
Gift to the world
I am a
Gift to myself
I am
Confident
I am
Creative
I am
Magical
I am
Beautiful
I am
Unique
I am
Loveable
I am
Valuable
I am
Enough
I am
Protected
I am
my Purpose

I am a unique being created by God on purpose. I am positive and optimistic about life. My cup is always full and always overflowing. I am special, talented and innovative. I am happily in love with myself.

Tierra Holmes

Appreciation

Appreciation

Should be shown on a regular basis
It should rise and set with the sun
It should be nestled in every handshake
It should energize every conversation
It should empower every hug and kiss
And it should be free for those who need it
Most...the ones who feel disposable

Ode to the Ghetto Black Woman

She is the fire engulfing the burning bush *or*
She is the fire *and* the burning bush

She is the Lamb given to the Gods *or*
She is the Lamb taken by the Gods

She is the sermon recited by her children *or*
She is sermon recited all alone

She is the hymn sung by angels *or*
She is the hymn sung to angels

She is the shortest last breath *or*
She is the longest first breath

Either way, she's here …

To Black Men

The power you possess is unimaginable
The need for your love is unfathomable
Our desire to be appreciated by you intensifies
Each and every time you enter our space...or leave
Whether by choice or by force

Remember, there's a seat for you here
At our table / the big one you helped build
With your broken hands and broken body

We see you collecting memories of lost knights
Collecting moons that once sat above your head
Counting stars plucked from your galaxy
Thankful and dismayed that it wasn't you
Feeling heavy with the life you still have

We see you walking, sometimes running
Towards the days when you had more control
When your life was simple / like rain water
A life force that cycles through the earth

Befriend us when you make your way back
Regenerate yourself with our family in mind
Remember the days we starved together
And appreciate the nights you spared small
Pieces of bread for your brother's children

Acknowledge your struggles and your strength
Call yourself a survivor and speak your candid truth
Strain your muscles until there's room for new growth
And find someone who can help mend your roots

Dance

Dance

Should be prescribed to the spiritually ill
To those in need of healing and understanding
Or to those who can heal others

It should be the gift regifted with pride
To those preserving community and self
Just as God preserves mother and child

It should be covered by all insurance plans
To help with depression and anxiety
Or to alleviate the burden of adulting

Dancing Apples (Excerpt)

Dance is an apple on a tree and I'm reaching for the ripest one to eat. It all began at the age of three when my big sister taught me how to extend my arms and seek the plumpest apple that could make my soul sing … And how to devour the fruity treat from its skin to its seeds just to make dance a part of my core being.

So, I dance. And when I dance, rejection and acceptance have no meaning. My spirit levitates and I vibrate on a higher frequency. Failure can't dissuade me from my mission or prevent my spiritual ascension. I'm deconstructing my existence through vulnerable self-expression.

Yet, there are times when I imagine life as thousands of deceptive pages within a book, and I fear flying my fingers down their narrow edges for a closer look or being punished for my inability to see that the dry brittle pages were often rude to me. Their sharp blades sliced each finger until they bled the blues. Apparently, I strummed too quickly for the truth.

So, on the ledge of my breaking point, I close the book and dance upon the desk, use anxious jitters to vibrate and phase through my fears, transform my inattentiveness into sparks of inspiration for short theatrical creations, engage my loneliness in conversations about community, and convert my dark days into playdates with God where He hides me, and I go seek me in places filled with…

Wholeness
Opportunity
Relationships
Tenderness
Happiness
Insightfulness
Naturality
Empathy
Soulfulness

& **S**erenity

And when I return to my personal space, I remember...I remember that when I dance, Imperfection is Queen. I have flaws and insecurities but I'm no mistake. I am understood and appreciated by the stage. I am reborn and I can breathe again. And I know in my heart that God gave me dance so my spirit could be released.

Stage Dance: A Dancealogue (Excerpt)

My soul was extracted, summoned by a black stage smiling but enraged, beckoning me to dance for a cure. Urging me to follow my Ancestors' feet and the cries of my unborn dreams, to envision a world where my womb is not a plantation and my creations are protected by the entire nation.

On this stage

My feet pound away at the base, making rhythms and music with the help of my legs. My hands clap and cap back at every attempt to enslave our joy — to enslave us. My body performs memories of rituals and prayers once the breath of our communities.

On this stage

America docked its boats, hung up its hooded cloaks, and settled in for a slice of Apple Pie. But our souls slithered into the trees, soil, air, water, and into then *their* memories. Now our blood is the pulse of humanity.

On this stage

My veins, throbbing and bobbing to West African, Black American, and Caribbean beats. My DNA, a sequence of black panthers, black griots, and black Orishas telling me to gather the blood, sweat, and tears drenching black slaves.

On this stage

I'm told to extract my truth and feed it to the people. To create a nutritious feast to revive the black lives eating gristle in the belly of the beast. I oblige without complaining and I know that dance is my birthright.

Tierra Holmes

Death

Death

Should be recognized for what and who it is
It should be invited to the dinner table
For a chat about our kinfolk on the other side
It should be offered a plate of our grandmothers'
Pineapple ham and ham rice, lamb chops smothered
In gravy, stuffed bell peppers, mac and cheese
(Without the sour cream), fried chicken, string beans
Black-eyed peas, and chitlins drowned in hot sauce
It should be asked to deliver a plate to them as well

Dolmen Passage Grave by a Sea
(An Exploration of Death/Examination of Life)

Buried deep, beneath
      Mounds of meditating earth
            Bodies wait for sun
Drops of murky wa-
      ter pinch their withered shoulders
            Puzzled eyes ask, "Why?"

Gentle banks entice
      Ribcages to consider
            Drifting across sea
Four chambers elope
      Circulating memories
            Above perfused hearts
Images of death
      Spiraling by as leaves   left
            Frozen and detached
Joyful acorns fall
      Slamming into Mother Earth's
              Fertile ovaries

The sea saw the moon
      Fully contracting her womb
              As new life emerged

Buried 3 Feet Deep

They were buried 3 feet deep, just enough to hide the soles of their feet but not enough to prevent them from breathing. Patiently, they waited for the day when their mother would unknowingly walk past their graves and sense their presence in the air. Their binkies, replaced with pounds of dirt, were the plugs keeping their mouths shut. Unable to wail or holler, their spirits called out to her. Crying her name, rattling their teethers, waving their white swaddles — they hoped she would recognize them, anything of them, even their smell. She did. She recognized their essence.

But would she believe her babies truly survived? Or was this another one of those days where clouds took the faces of her children? Sometimes smiling at her and giggling with bright eyes. Other times, frowning and blaming her for trusting a foreign God.

With that memory, she would remember the strength in her DNA. She would become a storm of flames unafraid to challenge the praying men who TWICE silenced her. She would remember the ways of her people, adorn herself in their protective spells, and pray for forgiveness (in advance). She would combust at the altar with his hands in hers remembering the ways of his sizzling touch.

Her pungent tears now the acetone trailing away from her babies' graves and to the doorsteps of worshipers who prayed that the innocent be unguarded. Fighting fire with fire, her screams of guilt and shame would make her tears catch flame. She could never unsee the burning or the touching. But she was not the first (or the last) arsonist.

She would inspire more babies, children, and youth to call out, to scream and shout so their people could find them. She would uncover the graves of many but the relatives of only a few. She would soak the bones — the ones that rattled her mind — in a cleansing prayer, clothe each one with love, and rebury them beneath her dancing feet. This time, the earth would keep them in peace.

Education

Education

Should belong to the people
It should be provided as a birthright
It should be delivered without bias or prejudice
It should be decolonized and re-rooted in culture
It should feed the mind and water the future
It should lift despair from the hearts of brown babies
And cleanse the soil beneath their feet

Sijo Needs to Know

Real confidence is not developed in a college class room.
Real life challenges are needed to strengthen your sense of self.
And when you believe in yourself, your self-esteem will grow.

Tierra Holmes

The Parent-Teacher Association (PTA) Meeting

Assembled in America's finest public schools
Learning to read their life sentences in English Comp
And tally their suspensions in Basic Math
Bundles of black babies, bugged eyed and manic, fight
For bits of polluted air hovering above their carnage
The superintendent wants to know, with all due respect

Where is their Ghetto Mother?

Teachers scribble notes onto a flyer covered with gold
stars and bright pink letters instructing attendees to,
"Stay 6-feet away", even the students in need of mending. They
ask the principal to call the nurse but he is not there. They all
want to know, with all due respect

Where is their Ghetto Mother?

Is she too busy to grace the school with her presence?
Will she arrive barefoot and bewildered...again?
Will she wear a bonnet as if she just rolled out of bed?
Will her loud voice scream for empathy we don't have?

Where is their Ghetto Mother?

Does she know that her southern drawl and slang trigger us?
That she embarrasses middle class blacks who have succeeded?
That she agitates white educators who just want to teach?
That she's too sensitive to the stares of black immigrants?

Where is their Ghetto Mother?

Are we to assume that she needs help?
Or can we proceed with the meeting?

It Didn't Add Up

She made space for me in her tiny office
cluttered with mountains of papers
perhaps assignments she meant to grade last week
or documents neglected over the past decade
about half the time she's been teaching *here*
at a black university for black students with a black past

She adjusted her glasses while reaching for her chair
It swiveled calmly in a circle just as my mind would
when she offered study tips on how to correct my speech
Not the equations that kicked out their legs and
tripped-me-up repeatedly in her class
Oh no, she wanted to teach me something else

Naively, I ignored her vibe and announced that *I* would
like to **ask, excuse me, ax** <u>Her</u> a question about the
formulas provided, the ones that made me sick
But before my question was constructed, she quickly
interrupted to shed light on what I really needed help with

"I want to tell you something that will help you. Because
of slavery, Black people say 'ax' instead of 'ask' and before
you go on an interview and they take note of this,
I want you to practice saying, '**A**ₐₐₐₐₐₐₐₐ**S**ssssssss**k**'."

Our exchange in those next moments revealed
<u>Her</u> vague connection with me, better yet, to me
To <u>Her,</u> being Jewish meant she cared enough about
this little black girl to stop her from speaking too freely

She gave me a dose of her ignorance and prejudice
but she also gave me something to proudly reclaim
something that I didn't know *we* did

29

Tierra Holmes

Family

Family

Should be redefined
It should include those folks
Who share dreams and values *if not blood*
It should expand our understanding
Of love and codependency so that we
Look to our broader communities
For acceptance and belonging

An Unspoken Contract

Below is an agreement between this one and that one, and that one and this one, and that one and that one, and this one and this one. They all speak, not to each other, but to the culture.

What Happens in the Home Stays in the Home:

    I.   Parents are not to be challenged
    II.   Children are not to be heard
    III.   Parents may fall from grace
    IV.   Children may take their place
    V.   Silence cloaks their tongues
    VI.   Guilt shatters their teeth
    VII.   Wisdom is extracted without sedation
    VIII.   Shame implodes upon detection
    IX.   You must suffer alone until everyone remembers, or until you forget. You shouldn't try to remember. It hurts.
    X.   You must use sex, education, and success to escape the moment. Never define the moment
    XI.   Only reconnect when Brother Grim summons a reunion
    XII.   Never confess to the black woman's fragility. She's never had a soft skull. Shake her. She can be shook – a lot
    XIII.   Use Fenty 498 to conceal your truth

Please sign below to accept the terms of this agreement (Note: you don't have a choice):

Signature: *The Bloodline*
Date: **Since Generations Ago**

Tierra Holmes

Fathers

Fathers

Should be exonerated
After being accused of imperfection
When their only crime was being human
They should be repatriated back to their families
And their roles should be clearly defined
So, they too can be proud of their contributions
For what is the purpose of men if all men are no good?

A Father's Love

Fathers bring their love wrapped in brittle blankets
firm, warm, and fragile

They hug their baby girls with pride and fear
Hide them in back rooms, away from harm
Lower them to the floor, away from the windows

For their baby girls, Fathers will work hours into
the night to provide light, enough to comb their
coiled hair, to brush their maturing teeth and to
read about foreign characters who know nothing
of their struggles

For their baby girls, Fathers will relinquish space
They'll bounce their baby girls on their bellies and
make room in their adult hearts for child's play
For their baby girls, Fathers learn quick that
chauvinism and arrogance poison Daddy's place

For their baby girls, Fathers board their hearts
disguise their blemishes, and weaken in solitude
Hoping their baby girls never understand they
are gravely vulnerable because they are black men

For their baby girls, Fathers will recite fairy tales
of endless triumph and success just to protect
their sense of security and to reject any limitations
of their ability to provide and to protect

But their lies aren't free from detection when
their baby girls are secret detectives who find clues
explaining why daddy's got the soulful, soulful black blues

They know daddy won't let them grow up, too
That he wants to keep them little, keep them safe
Keep them away from the windows and out
of harm's way by doing whatever it takes

A father's love can blind him to the truth, the truth
that his baby girl will experience her own blues
She won't always be satisfied or content
She'll experience some pain despite his efforts
to keep her safe

She'll trigger his hero instincts, and her own too
but deny him any rights to saving the day that
she wants to claim in her own name

She knows it's male fragility that warrants his shame
That makes fathers over-love their daughters and
accept the blame for any injuries they sustain

For their baby girls, Fathers need to realize
they are *only* men and that the love they wish
to gift should be thoroughly cleansed before
passed down to their children

That it should be gifted to themselves first
to guide their personal healing and then
regifted once they can identify what's missing
if anything at all

A Bucket for Your Tears

Dear Fathers,

Your daughters are ignorant to the challenges you face. Our
eyes are blind to the troubles you see. Our hands tremble with
the slightest weight of your burden. Forgive us for offering rest
 and poetry as solutions!

Your protection allows us to sleep peacefully at night.
Your sacrifices make it possible for us to cry in public. Your authority
frightens intruders. Your strength is our fortitude.

How dare we assume your suffering is an act? Or that your
tears enjoy the silencing effect of your pillows? How dare we
believe your fragility is non-existent despite the constant cracking
of your bones when you go to pick us up or to put us down?
Your little girls forgot or never knew their Daddies needed to
cry too.

But Fathers, please tell us, which basket is big enough to catch your
tears and to conceal the sound of their heavy drops? On what planet
can your daughters stand guard and defend your humanity? How do
we resurrect the innocence of your spirit and remind the world that
[you] belong here?

Please Daddy, please let us know.

Sincerely,
Your Baby Girls

P.S. It's okay if you're not sure.

Tierra Holmes

Hair

Hair

Should be celebrated
For the various forms it can take
It should be resurrected as a symbol
Of culture and identity protected by Title VII
Under the man-made and derogatory category of race
Our hair, whether long, short, kinky, or straight
Should be left alone, if not embraced
It should be set free, if not loved
It should be able to mind
Its own damn business
In peace

Water & Grease

Momma believed all it took was water and grease
To cultivate new growth and compliment her age
Simple ballies and barrettes would keep her daughter
Looking innocent but pretty enough for compliments
They would show the world her baby girl was loved
And that her Momma was worthy of respect

But when her Rainbow jeans no longer fit and her
Waist began to rock and twist, men ignored the
Pigtails and assumed she was buttered-up for them
Baby Girl with the big hips was no longer innocent
No longer a baby girl, just a girl with a baby face and
A coke bottle shape fresh enough for them to pop
Open and taste

When she finally got a perm, it confirmed (to them) that
She was old enough to date, old enough for *it* to not be
Considered rape. But even with the water and grease, she'd still
Be chased. "Cause, err'body know these young girls too fast
To stay in place!" At least that's what the community would say

And her age was more ambiguous after she learned their
Names, the dudes hanging on the street corners, the ones
Rolling dice at midday, dapping each other up, steady looking
At the young girls with the big Southern butts

And she spoke to them as if they weren't dogs in heat
Wide-eyed and gullible, she was a bird with clipped wings
Diving towards rough streets that provided no landing
The life lessons she once recited in a metallic cage were
Too wise and far-fetched for her to retain

Tierra Holmes

Baby Girl's blossoming coke bottle frame poured out any
Useful content in her brain and replaced it with compliments
From men who were obsessed with taking every last sip of her
Innocence

And Her Momma was naive to think that water and grease
Would prevent her Baby Girl from becoming a statistic
Everybody could tell, especially the men, that Baby Girl left
The nest a little too early and listened just a little too late
And it's shame that her hairstyle was to blame

Hot Comb

Living in her ears was the sound of
Hot teeth grazing her scalp and Blue
Magic Grease boiling into a runny goo
Her Mama said, "Girl, I told you not to move!"
The heat straightened her roots, discarded HER
Culture and devoured her confidence

Hair Love

What you'll need:
1. Water (in a spray bottle)
2. A rat tooth comb (for parting)
3. A wide tooth comb (for detangling)
4. Clips and sectioners (for keeping the hair in place)
5. Castor oil (preferably Jamaican Black Castor oil or Haitian)
6. Patience (for you and your roots and your tangles and your knots and your kitchen too)

What you should do:
1. Drench your love locs with fresh water
2. Drink from your scalp and not your ends
   (as you would from your mouth and not your lips)
3. Use black soap to wash away the stress of being black
4. Massage your crown with fingers that know their purpose
5. Condition your love locs with grandma's secret strength

6. Don't be stingy with yourself (give you what you need)
7. Detangle each section with care (no need to be rough)
8. Use the wide tooth comb for separating large sections
9. Use the tight tooth comb for parting small sections
10. Imagine your charting new pathways throughout your crown

11. Brush your parts with hemp oil and take a long, deep breath
12. Do some plaits or twisties and let your love locs dry freely
13. Be patient as you grow to know what love feels like
14. Repeat this process as often as you need

What you should remember:
1. Learning this routine will take time
2. You will often question what you need
3. Your roots and tips will always remind you
4. You *will* eventually feel the difference

Braiding on Glenville Ave

I sit on the stoop braiding my last two individuals
Two white women walk by, one from the left, one
from the right and I think to myself…
I don't crochet or sew — I braid
That's how I keep *my* hands busy

I look them in the eyes on the backs of their heads
keep my fingers firm, place one strand over the other
gently tug at my roots and-go-on *Braiding*

I speak to the ambiguous black brother bouncing on
his toes as he walks in my direction…His skin was the
color of honeyed plantains and his hair was like mine
a little looser, but   still   just like mine

He'd seen me early on, from about 10 feet away…My
presence was softer than the concrete beneath his feet
He was first to speak

He says, "HEY!!", as a smile breaks across his face
And I say, "Heyyy, how you doing?"
"Good!", he says,….. "I'm good."

I take note of the large, bulky chain around his neck
It was a deep, passionate red made of wooden circles
projecting and protecting his energy, something most
naturalists need in this country

He stops shortly after we speak to climb the stoop just
a few feet away…And I think, "This man lives next door
to me?" Now a smile graces my face
And I go-on *Braiding*

Tierra Holmes

Placing the end of the second braid between my teeth
I control the tension and protect my roots
On my temporary stoop, I turn my chin slightly left
then upwards towards the sun

I close my eyes and breathe in its warm rays with pleasure
My nostrils flare at the smell of old light are grateful
And I think to myself…I don't care if they see me or if they don't

I will enjoy myself and this stoop while it's mine
I will take my time and I will take my space
And I *will* keep my truth — it belongs to me

So, I go-on *Braiding*

He and Him

He and Him

Should be invited to speak
To share their experiences without being judged
To balance our narratives with their masculinity
He and Him should be viewed as misfits who
Are both feared and forgotten in our society
Because they can be

Young Bouls

Anywhere you look, a young boul is growing into a man
He's growing into his shoes and growing out of his pants
He's going through puberty and developing his voice
He's looking in the mirror, wondering if he made the right choice
Wondering if the girl he likes will notice him if he wears his pants
Sagging beneath his butt and his hoody over his head

One day, he'll muster up enough confidence to say
"Yo, Wussup?" "Hey, how you?" Or, "What's good?"
She may ignore him and decide, quickly, to walk away
He may stare at her for a while and consider calling her
Name, or calling her a bitch just to silence is friends who
Are laughing and crying at his "lame" attempt

Embarrassed, he may take this same energy to another
Young girl and assume she'll diss him like the last one did
Instead of being polite and kindly asking for her number
He'll point out her thin edges and critique her cheap outfit
He'll take her silence as disrespect and call her U.G.L.Y
An uncomfortable looking, goat-faced, lame-ass, young boul

In the moment, he may feel vindicated for his behavior
Hell, he may even laugh and smile in this poor girl's face
But, deep down, he'll know he wasn't raised that way
Deep down, he'll know that his pride was hurt
When the girl he liked didn't like him in return

So, I say to the young bouls:
A 'No' isn't a 'No' to your worth, just the situation
Rejection can be disappointing but you must be patient
Self-respect is when you love you despite what they say
She's not interested in dating you and that's okay
Your value is based on the quality of your character
And not the number of girls you can accumulate

Is it Meaningless to Hope?
A Young Boul's Soliloquy

Hot as ever in these summer streets. Mom's talking to Aunty 'bout dere bein' no food to eat. Lil brother walkin' 'round lookin' crazy. My big sister pregnant wit' her seventh baby. And Ah'm just sittin' here waitin' for sah'um to jump off. Cause Ah got a chip on my shoulder and daring sumbody to brush it off! Tha hotter it gets, life is worst for us all. Bullets pouring like raindrops, you can see tha bodies f a l l.

Pops always say, "They out dere shooting again!" And Ah say, "These bullets don't sleep. Tha trigger stay ready for any niggah bringing beef! Or any niggah too slow to dodge the heat! " Err'day it's tha same thing and Ah never know if tha next bullet is for me. Ah can be in North Philly, Uptown, Downtown, Old City! These bullets don't discriminate and the trigger ain't sweet. Parents' already digging kid-sized graves, and mine definitely got one ready for me.

Sometimes, Ah be thinking 'bout those soul snatchers, 'bout those body catchers. Ah be wondering if the adrenaline makes them clench their teeth? If they ever think before pulling the trigger, before seizing the life out these niggahs? Ah wonder if they dream of cold bodies crashing through the pavement and into their minds, begging and pleading for their lives? Ah wonder if they keep the bullet shells as trophies and sit them on their dressers for their folks to see.

Then sometimes, Ah be thinking, "Damn, that's some powerful shit!" Killing a niaggh, that is. You think of all dem lessons ya mom's done taught chu 'bout kindness and fairness, or 'bout them days ya pops told you solve your problems like a real man. But by 13, it's rare to meet a child without blood on his hands. These young shooters know they ain't gotta touch tha boul. They be standing 10 feet away, and just like that (fingers snap), they murk tha boul.

Niggah, that's like being a god in the hood and damn near God himself! Makes you think all of us should aspire to be like dem lil niggahs. Cause those shooters, they the ones that sign our diplomas, they the ones they write our checks and control our next breath.

Shiiiiittt, watching them on judgement day, Ah forget to whom Ah should pray! Ah be waking up saying shit like:

"Dear Lord...
No, Dear Bullets...
No, Dear Niggah wit' the Gun,
Please spare me. Lead me by sight and not by faith, so Ah can dodge the heat when it get hot. Cause, in a Niggah, Ah do have faith that he will pull the trigger on any given day. So, Ah pray that you keep me out of harm's way. Amen. Inshallah. Ashe. Ashe."

That's the type of shit Ah be praying these days. Cause these scriptures don't speak to me or truly reflect what Ah feel. So, Ah be like, fuck a commandment! These streets still expect me to kill or be killed. And even with a closed casket, the aftermath gone be harder to conceal.

Even church ain't safe, if you really wanna keep it real. Like, why would Ah got to church if Ah can be shot in the pews? If Ah can stumble out with blood discolored shoes? If Ah can break bread and then be broken into pieces? Or if mah spirit gotta follow a weeping procession to the grave mah parents made? The plot perfect for mah teenage frame.

And Ah ain't the only one thinking that way. Just ask the funeral directors who view my body as currency. Or the niggahs who'd set me up to get clipped when we was best friends since kindergarten. And somehow, someway, Ah'm supposed to believe a niggah like me can really experience peace.

In what world?

Melanated Man

Black is his culture, the way he eats
The way he dances, the way he kisses
God's feet

He's a conscious black man with a crystal
black plan

Black to him is a perspective, a conversation
It's a pro-black argument, it's a declaration
It's a promise made long before he was born

He is a conscious black man with a crystal
black plan

Black to him is a stage, it's a platform
It's a circle of ancestors and villagers
It's a time for gathering the truth and
Discarding the lies

He's a conscious black man with a crystal
black plan

Black to him is the future, it's the black
Diamond given to his beautiful black wife
It's the black child sprouting from her black
Womb

Dark   Lovely   &   Beautiful

He's a conscious black man with a crystal
black plan

Inter-generational Healing

Tierra Holmes

Intergenerational Healing

Should be common knowledge
It should be illustrated in a children's
Book where parents can learn to read
Between the joy and the pain and teach their
Little ones what real love looks like

Kitchen Cleaning

Prepare a bucket of bleach water
Grab some rags from the bathroom
Use the white one to remove the dust
Use the green one for deep cleaning
Clean your pots with soap and a little
bit of bleach water for disinfecting
Line the cabinets with sections of the
Wall Street Journal and dry your dishes
With a clean towel from the closet
Put them away nice and neatly

Like she did

Use her hands and eyes to scrub every
Spec that doesn't belong in the space
Learn the minute your fingers will prune
Embrace the smell of bleach and the
Gnawing pain in your palms from scrubbing
Be picky about which memories you display
Leave the dirty ones in the dishwasher
Make cleaning your mental baptism

Like she did

Find your peace and solace in repetition
Find your power and control in routine
Understand how trauma soils the day
Degrease your body with Ammonia
Dispose acts of violence from your
Muscle memory and forget you'd ever
been hurt in this world or by this world
Pour bleach down the drain and let the
water runnnnnnnnnnnnnnnnnnnnn **hot**

Turn on the garbage disposal and hear
The empty sounds of blades and electricity
Wonder if they're strong enough to shred your
Doubt of a system that spun you in circles

Like she did

Open your heart each morning to a deep

C   l   e   a   n   ing

Meet the sun at your altar before breakfast
Write letters to your brother on his birthday
Invoke memories of the living and the dead
Light Jasmine incense to attract good spirits
Bless your water; make it holier-than-thou

Like she did

Dance a faithful dance with several obituaries
Pressed to your heart with youthful hands
Thank the glorious gospel for your salvation
Forgive the church for co-opting the Word
Love your light and forgive your shadow

Like she did

Convince yourself that peace is currency
Invite your children to laugh with you
Dismiss any suggestion that poverty is
An excuse for misery, and embrace the
Reality you know belongs to you in this
Moment

Like she did

Healing Hands

Healing revives the broken body
While old hand-me-down hands
Mend wounds with stardust

Innocent souls   mummified
Are now waiting for release

Mothers bird-bathing babies with
Their tears are looking for relief

Lovers kissing through blue flames
Forget that fire creates ash and dust

Spirits laughing at their ignorance of death
Are excited to make new friends

Healing hands revive the broken body
But wise teeth reveal no names

Holiday Grief Accompanied by the Blues

This inner dispute involves a heart and a hammer. One pounding in anger, the other laying heavy with grief. Both are deadweights wrapped in Christmas sheets. Too heavy to press. Too heavy curl. Love bleeds through. Too abundantly to accept. Too frightening to embrace.

So, you must sleep with one eye open and all mouths shut. You must never say, "I love you.", unless you want to be blundered to death by a beating heart.

Give no presents this year. Frame your anxiety and send it back to your family. Remember blood is thicker than water but water rids the mess and hides the evidence.

Despite your depression, smile for the camera. Take the nearest exit from your relationships. Don't you dare pull the fire alarm! People will come and see you need help.

Go on the run. Bring only one bag of clothes, the ones with the least amount of stains. Hitch a ride to nowhere. Sit in the passenger seat and stare straight ahead. Give an alias that depicts a happy woman. Something like Gale or Aida! Maybe, Felicia.

Don't fall asleep. Remain awake crying with your eyes wide open. Clench your fists, your toes, your abs, your triceps. Glue your shoulders to your ears. Embrace the tension, and DRY YOUR TEARS BEFORE. THEY.
        F
            A
                L
                    L !
Tell the driver your life story. Omit the part where you ran. Play nice and happy, always nice and always happy.

When you arrive, treat yourself to dinner. Sit in the chair closest to the happy families. Order a blue rare steak. Don't worry, you won't get sick.

Use your weight to cut it. Chew on it for 15 minutes before pain gets stuck between your teeth. Ask for a toothpick! A broken one! Remember, brokenness keeps you company.

Stand up. Wiggle and pull down your skirt to adjust the length. Pay in cash — provide a 20% tip. Leave the doggy bag. You won't need it. Call a Lyft to your nearest destination — nowhere.

Debate with the driver about where nowhere is. Assure him it's a real place, a place you've been and are now going. After he demands that you, "Get the fuck out!", slam the car door and kick his tires. Remember...this nigga just called you fucking crazy.

Walk up the hill towards the wooded area. Sit on the nearest curb. Dial your sister — tell her you can't make it. Return home however you can, climb into bed and unravel your deadweight(s). Put on your silly Christmas hat and PJs. Make a bloody Bloody Mary with Jesus crowning at the brim

Pray He's born healthy. Pray He's the chosen one. Pray He finds you floating on the 41st day BEFORE. YOU.

D
R
O
W
N

Eat Before Dinner

She arrived to dinner with an empty stomach
Scanned the room with sullen eyes and a timid
Tongue before seeing a secluded table with her
Name resting in its center

She faltered toward an open chair, then hesitated to sit
Wondering if her hips would flow over the wooden plank
Holding her own hand, she inhaled an old compliment

"You're beautiful and intelligent."
        Then, she exhaled her true fears,
                "I'm unlovable and easy to abandon."

She sits…mesmerized by the silverware and its radiance
Remembering the wooden utensils gifted by her mother
She fondles them in her purse and then overheard the
Chandelier giggling at **Her Roots**, laughing at the way
Her shoulders
                d r o o p e d

She sits…a lighthouse in murky water, beckoning visitors
to spare their time and treasure her life like fine wine
to recognize her distance from the raging shore
to explore her truth with curiosity and not disdain
to remember her longing eyes fluttering in the rain and
to cherish her cracked foundation as growing pains

She sits...a modern faucet rusting from within
Spitting black drops of grimness onto the dishes
Filling clean cups to the brim with guilt and sin
Clearly, she's still healing and it takes more than
A fancy meal to create a new you, someone ready
To be treated like royalty

Joy & Happiness

Joy & Happiness

Should be free to keep and free to give
They should be exempt from taxation
Permitted to exist without consequence
Encouraged to thrive beyond the 9-5
And incorporated into our daily lives
As tools for survival

What is Joy?

Joy is when your mother gives you an extra 10 minutes to play outside.

Joy is when your father goes to sleep after you remind him, the 1st time, that his work is finished.

Joy is when you dance and your body feels free from discrimination.

Joy is when your sister-friends remember your birthday before you do.

Joy is when your braids aren't conflicted and each strand gracefully weaves into the other.

Joy is when you have just enough edge control left to style your baby hair.

Joy is when your brothers feel safe and comfortable enough to laugh in society's court.

Joy is when babies stare at you because they know you and not because they haven't seen your kind before.

Joy is when you learn your love language and can request it on demand.

Joy is when you open your fridge and see food.

Joy is when you realize you've been forgiven.

Joy is when you accept you as you are.

What is Happiness?

Happiness is when you quit your pre-designed life and find a new one.

Happiness is when you embrace your rented room as a blessing.

Happiness is when you feel free from responsibility and obligation.

Happiness is when you reject the problems of other people and deal with your own.

Happiness is when you sleep for hours into the work day and past your shift.

Happiness is when you lay on your carpeted floor and watch old movies.

Happiness is when you realize you own enough of your life to be free.

Happiness is when you believe you're loved even behind bars.

Happiness is when you live simply and enjoy moments of doing nothing.

Happiness is when you give two-fucks about titles, status, and prestige.

Happiness is when you become the CEO of your destiny and allow God to write your mission statement and vision.

Breaking Ice

As a little girl, I loved chewing ice. My mother says this is a habit I picked up from my paternal aunt whose loyal companion was always a cup of crushed ice. Although, my aunt didn't sit me down and say, "This is how you do it, niece." I somehow shared this joyful habit with her, and I loved it.

Overtime, I even found other creative ways to break clumps of ice into small pieces, making it easier to chew. One way was by taking cubes of ice from our freezer, wrapping them in a shirt (clean I assume) and banging it against our concrete floor in the basement. Or, I would slam the now damp ice pouch against a sharp corner of a wall, hoping my mother didn't hear the noise. At some point, I realized a hammer was more efficient because it immediately turned the cubes to slush. But the hammer reduced the amount of fun I could have from banging and throwing the ice against hard surfaces while quietly wishing that none of the icy gold escaped...or that my mother caught me crushing ice again.

Not once did I consider letting the ice melt a little before crunching down — that method seemed (and felt) too uncomfortable, too long, and too boring. On hindsight, I was only impatient with the process that was most uncomfortable, not slow, just uncomfortable. As an adult, I'd compare this to forming healthy relationships with ourselves and others. It can be time consuming, awkward, occasionally uneventful, and uncomfortable mostly when we can't predict the outcome.

Luckily, I'm at a point in my life where I'm willing to commit to a process or group of people simply because I want to. I'm not as obsessed with the end result or how I get there, so long as I have some moments of joy and happiness along the way.

Tierra Holmes

Love

Love

Should be sweet and sticky
It should be the red juice stain
On your white kitchen floor
It should be obvious to spot but
Much harder to remove
It should be the dried syrup
Sticking to your favorite plate
It should be the glue causing
Two hearts (or more) to conjoin

When a Poet Tries to Write about Love

What words must a poet use to describe her love?
What rhyme scheme must she employ to rock the reader's boat?
How efficiently must she illustrate her literary technique?

What metaphors and similes would best disguise her subject?
To what extent must she prove that her love was the latent need?
How in depth must she describe the romance before you believe
that *she* was worthy of being fucked?

When can she admit to the duplicitous nature of loving
one's self only after your love is given to another?
Around what time can she arrive fully naked?
In what font should she confess to throwing her love into
the gas chambers?

On what day can she retrieve her love lashes from church?
To whom can she disclose the status of her virginity?
By what time will she be released from judgement?

From whom must she secure validation?
Through which process must she galvanize her admirers?
At which moment can she disregard the rules and serve
the people raw truth?

Triolet 4

Beating your heart with love, I see me
Searching for a pulse that's happy
Expecting an answer with glee
Beating your heart with love, I see me
Watching our loving memories flee
And your tone grow cold and snappy
Beating your heart with love, I see me
Searching for a pulse that's happy

Waiting for Love

The phone will ring
once you're waiting
for yourself and not
for unrequited love

The phone will ring
when your flesh de-
cays and bees make
honey in your carcass

The phone will ring
once you preserve
your heart, feed it to
your children, and for-
get about the caller

Genuine Foliage

She is worthy of your love
Worthy of your fancy
Worthy of your interest and admiration

She is worthy of your time
Worthy of your respect
Worthy of your patience and devotion

She is worthy of your trust
Worthy of your loyalty
Worthy of your pride and protection

She is worthy of your support
Worthy of your appreciation
Worthy of your praise and gratitude

The question is: "Are you worthy of hers? "
Because, Love leans toward reflections of the sun
And longs for those who nurture her growth

Her Knees welcome cool kisses
Her Mind welcomes stimulation
Her Lips welcome conversation
Her Hands welcome sweaty hugs
Her Hugs welcome respect
Her Respect demands authenticity

She's ready to spring up when called
To decorate the family walls with
Her joy and reckless laughter

She's ready to brighten the family room
With her warm light and invite your
Eyes to open wide and see all of her

She's ready to crack open the family window
So, the cool breeze can tap you on the head

She's ready to enter the family kitchen
And prepare sweet memories with
radiant recipes

She's ready to fall heart first into your
Warm hands and be perfused, eternally,
With your electric energy

Love is ready to be loved
Genuinely and patiently

And when it comes to PDA
There's no hiding her affection
If physical touch is your love language

She'll hold your hands or nuzzle
Your cheeks and calmly say,
"You can kiss me."

Tierra Holmes

Mental Health

Mental Health

Should be invited to the cookout
It should be re-introduced to Nanna and
Everybody else who thought it was a fraud
It should be allowed to sit at the old folks' table
Where it can speak freely about the crazy cousin
Who was fed crazy by other crazy people in the family
And it should be taken seriously when it proposes
A new understanding of what crazy actually means

The Beginning:
Speaking Beyond the Grave

Our personalities developed in response to something OUT of our control, and fixed themselves *permanently* in our lives. We pleaded over and over, and over, and over again to have our sanity back! But, we never got it back. We learned to live without it. We learned to live without people.

People reminded you of things you wanted to forget and avoid. Avoiding the discussion helped you bury the problem, but only from the neck down. Deep down, parts of you needed to live above ground. Subconsciously, you watered split versions of yourself that craved fresh air and sunlight, versions that would keep their hands raised until you called on them, or until they grew restless and called out.

You heard them fighting for your attention, as you planted seeds elsewhere. You heard them breaking through the soil and crawling towards your dreams. You heard them speaking at the dinner table whenever you lowered your spoon for more peas. You heard them flushing the toilet when you grabbed water from the kitchen. You heard them confess and co-sign that you were the true imposter.

And you wondered how the deceased could speak from six feet under. You wondered if you left too many air pockets or forgot to cure the cement. You wondered if keeping the shovel was the reason you had nightmares, or if parts of you had truly survived.

And if parts of you did survive, why didn't you recognize them? Why didn't you see them as being parts of self? Why didn't you identify with them? Why didn't you console them? Why did they need consoling? Why did they need a place to stay? Why didn't you make room for them? Why didn't you introduce them to your community?

…. Why did you bury them a second time?

The Process:
Inner Disputes

The lower self often squabbles with the higher self; the two argue like siblings. At times, the lower self wins allowing our weaknesses to override our faith and confidence. At other times, our higher self prevails allowing us to envision a happier ending. But these weaknesses fuel our insecurities and help them morph into new fragments of our identity. Our lowest self is the blueprint, it's how we replicate our insanity until survival requires physical and mental shapeshifting. But when shapes are in motion, we can't identify the original.

It's pretty difficult. Trust me, I've tried! To hide from one's self is easier than confronting the pain that's inside. Especially when one of you is attached to a traumatic experience. That is, the you that you may never see again, unless you learn to silence the others and be led to that place where your painful memories have frozen over. At that time, all you can do is live through the confusion as you thaw. Slowly but surely, you will see it all. And the process has to be slow. Adding salt or warm water would cause germs to grow on your breast and thighs. Then you'll be stuck with another problem you'd want to hide.

During this process, you need to give proper attention and learn the events that made you cold. Or, you'll collect old habits and store them in the new you, the one that wants to be healed. So, yes, no matter how trivial or profound, the pain has to be re-lived experience by experience. And you must submit to the process of breaking the ice that conceals your true identity.

Poverty

Poverty

Should come clean
It should confess in an open courtroom
Reveal the truth about its criminal origins
And name the names that contributed to its existence
Down to the single sperm and egg united by greed

It should come clean about its dark humor and investors
About how it enjoys watching the plight of the poor
And the ascendance of the rich who sleep in guarded vaults

It should admit to the way it feeds starving comedians
With scarcity as if their laughter grows golden with suffering

ZIP CODES

Imagine
Poverty creates a map about where she's been and with who. And as whores do, she gives a rundown of all the men she left broke, all the girlfriends she cursed, and all the babies she aborted at Planned Parenthood.

Imagine
She spends the night counting food stamps like monopoly money, bragging about all the government cheese she received for her impoverished babies, and how she buys the rest of their food at the local Dollar Tree.

Imagine
She cares very little about quality or where they feed. She erodes the utensils and dishware instantly. She says, "They can eat out of their hands."

She doesn't care where they lay their heads, where they bathe, or where they find relief. She says, "They can sleep on the box spring. They can share the same bath water. Hell, they can shit in the same bowl. Just don't come complaining to me." And with a shitty hand, she passes out toilet tissue and magazines about the birth of poverty.

Imagine
Of all the places this bitch could have landed, she decides to land here. She gets comfy, hikes up her feet, and swears that she's clean. She lures in all the men and women she wants to fuck over. She fills their egos to the brim, makes them greedy, and seduces them with fake luxuries.

Imagine
Despite their empty pockets, she makes them spend. She morphs into expensive shoes, clothes, jewelry, knock-offs, and vacations — you

name it! Then imagine the bitch devours them, leaving a trail of
pennies that amount to nothing.

Imagine
She tells impressionable women that since Lincoln fucked her
ancestors, her pussy is ancient copper. That they should *want* to cop her
for a quick taste and a quick smell because she's been with the best.

Imagine
This bitch is wicked. She entices young children to play month-long
games of hide-and-go-seek by turning off their electricity. She ignores
the grace period and spits in the faces of their desperate parents.
Parents who starved so their children could share a teaspoon of peanut
butter.

Imagine
On Sundays, she attends the late service. While horny and hungover,
she criticizes church goers for being stingy. Invoking confusion and
strife among believers, she says, "You ain't too broke to give to the
Lord. So, you ain't too broke to give to me."

Imagine
She opens her mouth full of angel white teeth, smiles at married men
and shuns their wives. She claims to be a demon looking for God, and
asks, quite shrewdly, how she can find the light. Her blackness
swallows any ounce of sunshine and transforms warm souls into ice.
But they don't know this.

Imagine
During winter, she hoards rotten food in her pantry and pissy clothes
in her basement. She opens the windows facing your home and cuts on
the fan, knowing you'd long for the taste of fresh food and the smell of
clean clothes. But all you ever wonder is when she'll be evicted because
others had been evicted for less.

Romantic Revelations

Romantic Revelations

Should be useful

They should bring good fortune and wisdom
They should be relevant to experienced lovers
And intriguing to new lovers curious about Love
They should confirm that romance is an illusion we
Embrace with our bare breasts and stripped minds
And they should explain how we still found love

After so many left turns

Vintage Love Letter

you have been a flower, the most precious flower one could pick. with each petal i pluck from you, with your consent, i learn a lesson about myself, one that only you could teach. i admire your beauty. you grow each day. whilst sitting in the sun where my petals are not as bright, colorful, or innocent, you invite me to join you. you invite me to sip your water for nourishment, even if it leaves less for you.

you share your space with me: you tell stories of your past, present, and future. you tell stories of your family. you speak of them with pride and humility. and i wonder which relative planted you.

each day you arch your spirit a little closer towards the sun, away from the cold darkness. you absorb power from the Most High and create the brightest colors your spirit could ever share with the world.

you live in soil: The Blackest Soil, the most resistant soil, soil that gave birth the 1st revolution. you speak honorably of the country whose soil captured and packed within your mother's womb. you germinated in that soil — it lives within you. it covers you as a cloak. it shields you and provides _ _ _ _ _ _ _ _ _ a trail back home, back to where it was grasped by your parents' green hands.

one day, you will have to return and collect the same soil **rich** in history, **rich** in resistance, and **rich** in blackness. you will have to return and make space for your own creations, for your own dreams and seeds. but you already know this. you're prepared for this.

you welcome new lessons as much as you teach them. you pay attention to details. you speak freely of love and resilience. you are unconditionally rooted in the community. you pay homage to the elders both breathing and sleeping. you safeguard the new spirits walking this earth.

you deserve to be planted in a garden of your own kind. you deserve to be watered daily, freely, and lovingly without condition. you deserve to be happy. you deserve freedom. you deserve to look back on your life knowing your generosity was appreciated!

i was not there to see you planted. i was not there to see your stems grow and replenish but i see you now. and i hope to trace the shape of you, to write notes about the fine details i see within you, and to preserve every moment with you.

i hope to learn where you fit within the pages of my life. so i meet you where you are and i sit at your feet. i hope you drop hibiscus petals into my diary and color me a rich pink.

and i hope to learn what you are here to show me and what i am here to show you.

Sailing on Your River

Sailing on the
r i p p l e s
of your river
pull! pull! pull!
Do not push me away

       Bring me closer to
       the core of your heart
       where I wish to stay

          Splash me with your kisses
          Drench me with your love
          Make me wet with your hugs

          Your river is the bluest
          diamond my eyes have seen
          No lake, no ocean, no pond

      or creek could steal my
      attention from your
      current's flow

    Let me flow with you
    I would never build
    a dam to control you
    Whichever way the

Wind blows, let the breeze
open your eyes to me as I
wet my feet on the banks
of your love

Intention

We trust when we should let go

This man entertains himself with
The confused woman; she's a victim
In his game

Fidgeting with the control stick
She doesn't know which button
Can make him jump and kick

We trust when we should let go

His narcissism, satiated by her
Bashfulness creates a dangerous
Environment…..for her

We trust when we should let go

With blind faith, she dances too
Close to crocodiles, feeds black
Bears with her bare hands, feasts
Alongside Hyenas, sleeps with
Mosquitoes, meditates with Horse
Flies and prays beside the Fallen Light
She has molded her fate tonight

We trust when we should let go

Relationships

Kisses
memorize the
taste of lipstick

        Firm
        grips imprint
        love stains on hips

                Bandage
                your wounds
                Blood has no place
                in the rainbow

Cover Paige

Peter married Paige
Paige, he married her
To Paige, he was married
Her love was vital to his health
But she trotted around the globe
Without a moral guide or a map

There was a time when Paige landed
In South Africa and proclaimed her
Love for Peter each and every day
She even dined with his photo
Opposite her candle lit plate

And her earrings were prized possessions
For they were engraved with *his* name
Every excursion in Cape Town led to
Daydreams about her Lover's sweet
Kisses and his manly chest mane

Paige wrote to Peter faithfully after morning prayer
Her letters were both descriptive and elegant
She mailed each of them without delay
But one day, she would pull out a blue pen
And assess what she really needed to say

She was having visions of a new life
One more exciting without him in it
And she refused to write another chapter
Based on his personal dreams and wishes

So, she mailed Peter his last letter, this time
Without leaving her scent on any page
She ran to the foot of Table Top Mountain
Asking the winds to help her climb it again

Sexuality

Sexuality

Should be vindicated
She should receive apologies from the hypocrites
Who blame her for their ungodly thoughts
Who detest her in public but praise her in private
And who deny any affiliation as if she's a sin
She should be christened with womb water
And hung in church to dry beside her Creator
Long enough for her stress wrinkles to smoothen
And long enough for the holier-than-thou to confess
To wearing her out for days on end

The Thoughts of Peeches

Is it wrong to say I fucked him on the first night? What's so shameful about fucking, especially when I'm a grown woman with grown woman problems and grown woman needs?

Should I omit the part where *I* asked him to come upstairs? I've always wondered why upstairs was code for bedroom and bedroom was code for bed and bed was code for fucking. What's wrong with just asking someone to fuck? Whether it be outside, on the stoop, in the backyard, in the car, on the table, in the pews with the collection plate dude, what's the issue?! Please tell me.

Should I deny giving my consent while intoxicated or demanding he moan each syllable of *my* name, both forwards and backwards? I've always wondered why women were expected to moan like cats in heat. It's as if people think we've never had dick! Well, someone of us haven't. Some of us don't like it. But the point is, the dick ain't doing nothing we can't do for ourselves. And see me, I'm actually the one who makes the men moan, LOUDLY, without restriction. And I give them permission to stroke my ego with the quickness.

But society has a way of draining your creative brain and robbing you of your audacity to be free. Yet, the question remains: Why can't I, a "woman", talk freely about fucking? No, I'm not promiscuous! I'm not a slut, a whore, or a "bad girl." I simply challenge the role forced on me and give myself permission to think! I embrace my sexuality in private and in public regardless of who has something to say.

Prostitute Called Liberation

Sensual creature I am
Bounded by hands molding my moans
Shaping my breaths / stressed / unstressed
My bra, a deep money green, digresses to the floor
But I'm no whore — we're married to sex
We took an oath to love, fuck, and protect
Preferably until orgasms take our last breath
We read our vows on an old couch filled with
Memories of naked bodies bouncing on its springs
There was nothing to fear and nothing to explain
So, we moved forward with doing our own thing
His fingers slipped into my bedazzled pouch and
Unzipped hidden spots I never knew existed
Compartments originally meant to be kept a secret
I was told they whispered to him, captivated his attention,
Hypnotized his mind, and made his bones shiver
My secrets imprisoned him, gripping his thick limbs
As they eagerly extended, disconnecting truth from fiction
Then it was my turn to find where his secrets lied
I found a gem worth polishing all night with wide eyes
And open hands ready to embrace his angelic souls
As they don't quite know where their journeys end and
Neither of us know if we're dreamers in need of a pinch
I squinched when he tickled my narrow neck
He checked my breathing before he flinched on his back
Our movements were making such beautiful music
Our muscles contracted in unison dancing to the tunes
And the truth is we were fucking sixty-nine illusions but
It was my sweet solutions that brought us back to earth
No longer were we confined to the wishes of the world
And this is why he called me *his* Liberation

Sisterhood

Sisterhood

Should be second nature
It should be expected from women and girls
Who value togetherness and collective strength
It should be shared between mother and daughter,
Mother and grandmother, mother and granddaughter
And all those who attribute their collective magic
To the bread they broke for many nights

Sister

Had I known you before that day
I woulda asked for your name
I woulda invited you to play

Had I known you before that day
We coulda become best friends
We coulda been just like twins

Had I known you before that day
We shoulda hid behind her rib cage
We shoulda laughed and cried with rage

Had I known you before that day
I woulda co-signed your name and
Taught you all the rules to the game

Had I known you before that day
I coulda asked mom for extra time and
Bought us candy with a few nickels and dimes

Had I known you before that day
I shoulda made them listen and see
That you clearly had a vibrant heartbeat

But I didn't get to know you at all
Seems like big sisters were never called for
Their opinions or to share genuine feelings

Meanwhile, your lifeless birth was
Still a new beginning / She spoke of you
Often, as if you were once among the living

And to this day, I believe that you were the little
Girl borrowing my toys and making them blink
Remaining invisible to the family but never to me

Baby Girl....Remember This

Nothing in this world
Can dim your power, except you
You're Gorgeous and Divine
You can be anything in this world
that you choose

You are Light, Beauty, and Innocence
The only way is up! Just focus your mind
On loving yourself

You are Brave, Kind, and Strong
What tried to bring you down must
NOT have known!

You are POWER and RESPECT
You're the bridge to your own success
Cause your sisters got your back!

You are the dream we see
The mission we must protect
by any means

Without your presence, our circle
Is incomplete and depleted of
Our magical black girl energy
Cause I am you and you are me

So, Baby Girl
Little Princess becoming a Queen
Never forget *our* legacy because
You are the future your sisters need

Rosy Red

Wherever she goes, men drop to their knees
Kissing her toes, pedicuring her feet
They love her look, her style, her way of speaking
For she is a woman only captured in their dreams

This slender body beauty with bouncy red hair is
Ideal. Her confidence is a sun that never sets. Her
Beauty is a star that women wish upon, or at least admire

And she speaks with a rose peddled tongue
Until it becomes thorned with the truth
She often pricks her lips licking clean the wounds
Truth be told, like any other woman, she has doubts
Insecurities too

Beauty cannot exempt her from love's pain and
Admiration cannot shield her from rejection
Based on our strengths and our weaknesses, we
Appear to be the same

Yet, she is still she and I am still me
We're two beautiful beings with our own meanings
Our sisterhood makes us synonymous

Tierra Holmes

Sugar-Coated Shame

Sugar-Coated Shame

Should be called out
It should be held accountable
For its impact on our health
It should be found guilty of
Murdering the spirits of vulnerable
Souls — both young and old
It should be forced to explain
Which incentives make life worth
Living when silence has a sweeter
Taste than community healing

When They Ask for More

They stand, their eyes polished with tears and hatred
Their hands empty and pride full
They questioned you   for
Leaving their bellies desperate and their spirits torn   for
Shattering a legacy before they were born   for
Making trauma and grief a traditional feast
They stand, their eyes a vacant lot accusing you
Of endangering their lives with your absence
And destroying their spirits with your presence   Now
You come to their pine boxes empty handed
Offering your excuses instead of condolences
Embracing mourners with quivering lips and a petition
For blind unity as if you didn't know blood
Isn't' as thick as abandonment and thieves can't return

what was stolen

Tierra Holmes

Acknowledgements

The purpose of this section is to give thanks to specific people who helped me during this process.

First, thank you to the divine energy within me that clarified my purpose and guided my words throughout each poem. Thank you to every character explored within these narratives — both real and imagined — who made an impression on my life and inspired me to create meaning out of moments.

A special thank you to my mother who was the first writer and poet I ever met. Thank you for sparking my interest in this art form, for listening to me ramble about my challenges and successes, for reading and then re-reading my work, and for giving me permission to share our collective truths. Thank you for your honesty, critical feedback, and questions. Our conversations helped me reflect on my intentions and strengthened my understanding of self.

Thank you Josephine A. Pokua, my sister-friend, for following your dreams and self-publishing your first chapbook. The timing of your book was significant because I was in the process of reflecting on my goals and remembering that I, too, dreamt of being a published author. You were a resource in so many ways: answering *all* of my questions about self- publishing, critically reviewing sections of my book, and for seeing me as I am. Thank you being there when I needed you.

Thank you Sytonia Reid, another sister-friend, for understanding how important this project was to me. Thank you for proof-reading my entire manuscript less than two weeks from my initial publishing date. I appreciate your eyes for catching all of the "mistakes" I missed and bringing them to my attention. Your selflessness and support increased my gratitude for you, and I'm thankful to have you as my *chosen sister.*

Thank you to Sekaya's Corner for providing a free consultation and tidbits on how to self-publish. Your positive words and encouragement made a difference.

Thank you to everyone else who assisted me throughout this journey. Your encouraging words and faith in me were pivotal during those days when I needed extra motivation. Much appreciation to those who read early drafts of my work and shared their unfiltered reactions. Your feedback made me realize that there *are* people out there who can relate.

Last but not least, thank you to the readers who purchased this book with an open mind. Your generosity and time are much appreciated, and I hope you find a story (or more) that resonates with you.

Thank you again,

Tierra

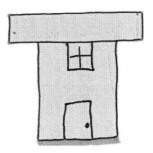

Holmes Publishing

Printed in Great Britain
by Amazon

75715592R00070